Situational Survival Guide:

20 Survival Strategies for a Dangerous World

The information herein is offered for informational purposes solely, and is universal as so. The presentation of the information is without contract or any type of guarantee assurance.

The trademarks that are used are without any consent, and the publication of the trademark is without permission or backing by the trademark owner. All trademarks and brands within this book are for clarifying purposes only and are the owned by the owners themselves, not affiliated with this document.

Table of Contents

Introduction: Be Prepared...5
Chapter 1: Dealing with Power Outages 6
    Solar Power..6
    Using Generators 7
    Wind Power 8
    Hydropower 9
Chapter 2: Surviving the Winter and Staying Warm 9
    Solar Hot Water Heater..10
    Window Solar Heating 12
    Using a Hand Drill 13
    Pack Warm Clothing and Blankets...14
Chapter 3: Finding Water in a Drought 15
    Using Rain Barrels..15
    Pull Water From Plants..16
    Dig Water From River Beds 17
    Get Water from Rocks 17
    Recycle Your own Urine...18
Chapter 4: Surviving an Earthquake..20
    What to do in the Immediate incidence of a Quake 20
    Stay Connected through Radio..21
    What to do in the Immediate aftermath of a Quake 22
Chapter 5: Self Defense and Surviving a Physical Attack...24
    Learn to React Fast...25
    Learn how to Block 26
    Learn how to Pack a Punch 27
    Aggressively Scream 28
    Psyche Out Your Assailant with a Running Attack 29
    Inflict Pain with Pressure Points..30
Conclusion: You can Survive 31
FREE Bonus Reminder 32

Introduction: Be Prepared

There is no situation on this planet that you cannot prepare for. No matter what the situation or circumstance you can be ready to face it without any problem. No what you need in order to make it through the crisis. Learn how to survive the storm, both literal and metaphorical. No matter what happens, everything is said and done; there is absolutely no reason why you should not be prepared. Follow the next few chapters closely and use them as your blueprints for survival, we live in some perilous times, so prepare for them!

Chapter 1: Dealing with Power Outages

In order to survive any given situations, the first thing you need to do is keep your eyes peeled. What does that mean? It means that you need to be aware of your surroundings at all times. Don't let anything surprise you. If a bad storm is headed into your area, or an earthquake is about to strike you need to know about it. In this chapter let's go over some of the best ways that you can stay informed during a power outage. We depend more and more on grid based electric systems to survive, but what if all the grids were to collapse on us tomorrow? What would we do? If we are in the middle of the winter and we can't rely on our electric heater, how would we stay warm?

Solar Power

Many are aware of the situation when it comes to the failing infrastructure of our city's grids, but most are not aware of how they can combat this precariously dire situation. Well, I have one easy answer for you; the sun. The sun has enough power to light up the entire planet for billions of years. That nuclear dynamo floating in space that we call the sun showers us with untold power every single day, we just have to know how to harness it.

There are many types of solar panels and solar collectors on the market right now; you just have to know which ones would be best for your situation. If you are not planning on living for extended periods on solar, you can bypass the full installation of solar power, in favor of portable solar charges. There are several of these on the market right now, and they are excellent for charging cell phones, lap tops, and other electronic devices.

Using Generators

For some of us, even if the whole city went dark, as long as we had our phone and laptop we would be fine, but sitting in the dark with just a phone and a laptop is not enough for many more, especially those whose families depend on electric heating and cooking. If you are facing extended periods of rolling blackouts then you may want to improvise some longer lasting solutions. One of these would be to get a generator. The often cited drawback of generators is the fact that they are too loud, too smelly, and sometimes too inefficient. But if they are maintained properly you can mitigate most of these annoyances.

Most generators run off of gasoline, diesel, or natural gas. Natural gas would be the best option for a home power system since it would create the least fumes, greatly reducing noxious odors. Natural gas is also easier to store, and unlike regular gasoline, it doesn't go stale after sitting around for an extended period. But if you are planning on getting the most electricity possible from your generator, you would have to go for diesel fuel. Diesel is the workhorse fuel for generators and in the end is the least expensive and has the longest duration for long term use.

Wind Power

If you live in a location that receives a ton of annual windfall, then you just may be well suited to benefit from wind power in the face of a blackout. Just put you're your wind turbine up and start collecting the wind. Wind turbines work like electric cooling house fans in reverse. As you may know, any cheap cooling house fan, works by plugging the fan into the wall, then hitting a power button to send the electricity from your wall to the fan causing a motor to spin the blades and produce wind.

But if you look at the way a wind turbine works, you have the complete opposite. Wind causes the blades of the turbine to spin, this then causes a shaft inside a generator to turn, which then produces energy that can be sent into the wall outlets of your home and *produce electricity*. The house fan is using electricity to create wind and the wind turbine using wind to create electricity.

Hydropower

If you live near a stream, river, or creek you very well could power your house with hydropower. Hydro power has the full potential of leaving you with a large amount of electricity with very little in the way of investment. There are just a few variables involved in determining just how much power you might be able to glean from your system. Number one you have to establish just how mush water pressure you can derive from what in hydro-speak is called the "head".

The head is the amount of vertical distance that your water source will drop down from and into your turbine. Having that said, you could have a micro-hydro turbine in operation from as little as 5 feet, but for optimum pressure you should have a head of at least 15 feet or more. This system will generate at least a moderate rate of electricity, for low residential demands, such as basic heating and lighting. As with solar and wind power, this energy can be stored in batteries for later use.

Chapter 2: Surviving the Winter and Staying Warm

Despite all of the theories and speculation of global warming and climate change, there are still parts of the world that are gripped in bone chillingly cold winters. And according to the latest news about the polar vortex this winter is supposed to be one of the worst we have seen in a while. Harsh winters can really shut down civilization, so we need to prepare for these contingencies. Among other things, we have to know how to stay warm in potentially frigid environments. Keep reading to learn more!

Solar Hot Water Heater

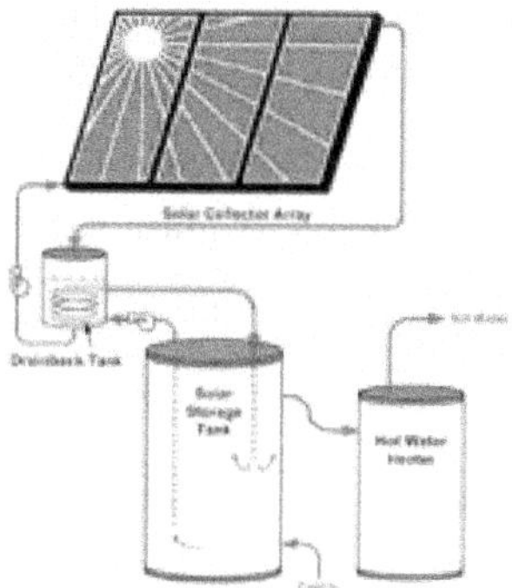

Even in the worst of winters, as long as it is not completely overcast, power can still be gleaned from the sun. And such is the case with solar heated water. Believe it or not, simply by painting a board black and allowing it to absorb the sun, you can have yourself a water heater. In order to construct such a device all you will need to basic component, a container for the heated water, and a solar collecting apparatus. Both of these units can be made from everyday items found in the house.

Start off by building your solar collecting apparatus. Just take a square piece of sheet metal and a similar sized cardboard box of the same exact size, some black paint, and copper tubing and gather them together. Once these components have been acquired, take out your copper tubing and bending it like an "S"" put it right on top of the sheet metal, making sure that it covers the whole breadth of the metal. Now get out a soldering gun and solder your copper tube in place. Next, paint the entire assembly of copper tube and sheet metal black.

After that, get out your cardboard box and cover the bottom and sides of it with insulation. Once you have done this, poke out two holes, with one on each opposing side (these are for your copper tube to poke out of), once these are in place put your painted black sheet metal and copper tube down into the bottom of the box with both ends of the "S" shaped copper tubing pointing out of the holes in the sides of the box. Put this assembly to the side for now and move on to the construction of your water heater.

Find an empty coffee can and drill two holes on each side of the can. Make sure that one hole is at least one inch from the bottom of the can's rim, and that the other one, on the opposing side is one inch away from the top of the rim. Run more copper tubing through these holes and solder them in place. Now simply get a good strong plastic tube and run it from the coffee can water heater back to the black painted solar collecting apparatus. Now when you fill your can with water, it will be instantly heated by the hot air blowing through the tubes of the solar collector. It may not be the most glamorous of contraptions, but this will give you warm water in the winter!

Window Solar Heating

Have you ever heard of a window air conditioner? Well, guess what? You can create a window heater which attaches right to your window, and blows in warm air, just like those old fashioned window air conditioners blow in cold air. The window that presents itself as the best candidate for this is the one that faces the south, this is due to the physics of the intensity of sunlight, and where it most efficiently will strike your home, which is always on the southernmost wall of your home.

After you pick out your window measure it and then go to a piece of cardboard and cut out the exact dimensions of what you have just measured. You can then use this to completely cover your window. But first get out some glue and use it to completely cover your board, next, paint the board completely black After you have done this, cut out 6 ventilation holes on the edges of your cardboard, with each of them about 1 and a half inches in length. Now just slip this specially painted piece of board into your window frame and let it start absorbing sunlight. The black coloring will attract sunlight and bring a great deal of energy.

Using a Hand Drill

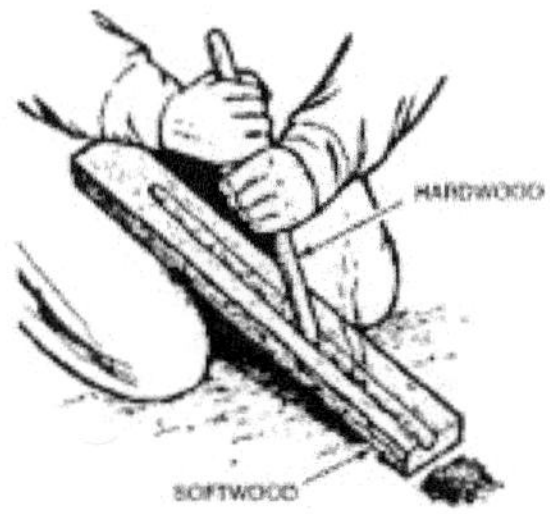

If you re stuck out in the freezing cold and you have no other recourse for your heating, in order to stay alive you just might have to quite literally, take matters into your own hands. Known as a "hand drill", this tool is ancient and has been used to spark up campfires for quite some time. The tool itself consists of stick about 10 inches in length and a wooden board, known as a "fire board" on which the stick the end of the stick is placed.

Stand this stick right up on the board with the bottom end pressed hard into the wood and then begin to vigorously move the stick back and forth in between your two hands. You should soon be able to catch a spark from the friction and start your fire. This will at least keep you warm during these desperately cold winter nights.

Pack Warm Clothing and Blankets

This one probably seems like a no brainer, but I have to mention it. When the temperatures drop make sure that you have plenty of blankets and warm clothing. Because remember when your mom told you to bundle up and where layers? Well, guess what? She was absolutely right! If you have to face the elements, you should where an undershirt, a long sleeved shirt, a sweater, a light coat and then a heavier coat on over that! But most importantly make sure you cover your head, 90% of all body heat goes right out of our old noggin! So make sure you put a toboggan (or any other kind of hat) on your noggin to keep from losing your precious warmth to the winter chill!

Chapter 3: Finding Water in a Drought

If you live in the western United States (or anywhere similar) then you know just how deadly droughts can be. They cause wildfires, and ruin the land, but much more than this they eat up the water supply. All of the land's surface water literally goes up in smoke, in the form of evaporation from being baked in the sun for way too long. But don't worry, this chapter is going to provide you with some ingenious means of producing water even in the most brutal of dried out, drought situations.

Using Rain Barrels

Droughts by their very nature are dry and lacking of rain. But in the off chance that rain does fall, you should have a rain barrel ready. Because even the worst of droughts can have random, sudden intermittent rain showers, so you have to be ready to capture what rain drops you can before they are all swallowed up by the dust. Rain tends to disperse over a wide range, so the wider your rain barrel's mouth the better.

Rain barrel's are usually large, round, wooden containers and can be found at most hardware stores. But even if you don't have a traditional rain barrel you can always improvise and turn a trash can into readymade rain barrel all of its own. Just take a standard plastic trash can, make sure you thoroughly sterilize it, and set it out in front of your house. It may not be exactly glamorous to drink out of a trashcan turned rain barrel, but it will keep you from being dehydrated!

Pull Water From Plants

You may not realize it, but all plants contain water. They are by their very nature, living water containers. So it would only make sense to try to tap into this water during a dangerous drought situation. You can collect water from plants through what is known as a "transpiration bag", which is basically just a small plastic bag that can be attached to plants in order to pull water from them.

You can just take standard freezer or sandwich bags and attach them to the plant. Just make sure that the plastic bag seals onto the vegetation nice and tight. Any condensation from the plant will then be perfectly sealed into the bag, unable to evaporate into the air. With this sealed contained bit of water, you have beaten the drought for good!

Dig Water From River Beds

Believe it or not, even under the veneer of a dry, baked, and cracked desert riverbed there is most likely some water locked under the surface. Just take a shovel (or any other utensil) and start digging down into the riverbed and after you reach a few feet down, you will have no doubt struck some water. At the very least you will come across some moist sand, and moist sand is nothing to balk at during a dangerous drought. If you are about to literally die from thirst, squeezing drops of water from muddy sand could save your life. It's not real image appealing to drink mud, but it does allow you to survive the situation!

Get Water from Rocks

If you thought getting water from plants and a dry riverbed was interesting, you haven't seen anything yet! Because you can also pull water right out of rocks! Even rocks strewn across a desert landscape usually have some water trapped inside of them. In order to get to this water you should take a regular household straw and stick it down into the cracks of the rock. Once in the cracks just start sucking up any water left in the rock.

Admittedly you have to be careful with this however, because I had a friend who once sucked up a spider trying to do this trick! And neither he nor the spider was very happy about it! I would just try to shake the rock a bit, and give it a good once over in order to avoid this. But when you get right down to it, if you are nearly dead from thirst, sucking a spider up would probably be the least of your concerns. So just in case, you are in such an incredibly dangerous situation, keep in mind that you actually can get water from rocks.

Recycle Your own Urine

I know how unpleasant this all sounds, but you can in fact recycle urine into drinking water. The vast majority of your urine is made up of the same H2O that you drank in order to create the urine in the first place, so as long as you filter out the intermittent waste products you can drink it. It's not pretty, but if there are

no other options, this survival strategy could save your life if you are in a dangerous drought situation.

The best way to recycle urine is through creating what is called a kind of active, solar filtration device. This is done by digging a hole in the ground and placing a plastic cup at the bottom of it. Once you have done this, put a piece of plastic tarp over the hole completely covering it. With the hole covered like this, no start pee-ing right over the plastic cup underneath, as the urine settles on the plastic cover-ing, it will begin evaporating in the sun. The remaining pure water elements will then sink down through the plastic and drip into the plastic cup below. It's not real appetizing by any means, but you can safely drink this filtered and recycled urine.

Chapter 4: Surviving an Earthquake

Deadly Earthquakes have been on the increase in recent years, and in some cases they have occurred abnormally far from known fault lines. Much of the world is at risk from these killer quakes, and you just have to know how to handle these dangerous situations. This chapter highlights some of the best ways to be prepared.

What to do in the Immediate incidence of a Quake

As soon as you feel the first tremors of an earthquake you need to take immediate action. This means you should find a strong structure such as a table to get under in order to shield yourself from any structural collapse. Also be sure to stay away from any windows so that shattered glass doesn't strike you.

Infrastructure may be frayed during a massive earthquake, but it doesn't necessarily have to disappear completely. Even though cell phone towers will most likely be non-operational, radio will be your best bet of sending and receiving information. In order to hear the latest bulletins about the situation as it unfolds all you need is a small battery powered radio that can pick up local radio stations.

These radios are cheap and highly effective, well worth the few dollars it takes to buy them, if it means staying updating about dangerous situations as they unfold. Radios are not only a means of one way communication either, because if you happen to have a Ham or even better, a C.B. radio you can communicate right back! Any good survivalist should have at least a bare minimum of radio equipment during an earthquake.

<u>*What to do in the Immediate aftermath of a Quake*</u>

As soon as the tremors die down and you have been given the all clear through a radio bulletin that the earthquake is over, you can congratulate yourself that you survived. But don't be fooled, because the danger is not over yet. Much of the infrastructure where you leave is no doubt in upheaval after such a massive earthquake and you need to be prepared for the aftermath. In your survey of the damage to your neighborhood you should especially pat attention to any hissing sounds that you may hear.

If you hear a loud hissing sound anywhere near your home after an earthquake followed by the smell of gasoline, then you need to get out of there immediately. Because that hissing sound is a sure sign that there is a gas line break somewhere in your vicinity. This is an extremely dangerous situation and if your whole home doesn't blow up, the fumes alone could be deadly, so get out of there as fast as you possibly can.

Besides checking for gas leaks, the next thing you should watch out for is any possibly short circuits in your electrical system. Before doing this however, make sure that you are free and dry from all moisture, so you don't get shocked. After you've made sure that you are nice and dry, turn off your circuit breaker and start looking at your homes wiring, making sure there are no broken threads. If you are sure that your wiring is intact, you can then turn the power back on. If you are ever faced with the dangerous situation of an earthquake, this is what you should do.

Chapter 5: Self Defense and Surviving a Physical Attack

As a kid whenever I complained about the school yard bully giving me a hard time, my dad used to always tell me, "Ok son, just don't let them get the best of you." This phrase is very wise when it comes to self defense, because essentially what it means is to never let your opponent overwhelm you to the point that you are completely powerless to stop them.

Because that is the strategy of most attackers, they want to catch you off guard and quickly terrorize you into submission with fear. Unless he is completely insane, no mugger in his right mind wants to have to fight tooth and nail over a wallet that might only have 20 bucks inside of it! Most assailants are looking for easy pickings that won't give the any trouble.

The last thing they want is someone who actually fights back. The second you fight back, you have all the momentum on your side and your attacker will be completely surprised by your ferocious rebuttal. Once you have the element of surprise on your side, don't let it go. Like my father always said, "Don't *let them get the best of you*." In this chapter learn some of the most ingenious self defense strategies that will allow you to do just that!

Learn to React Fast

The worst thing you can do when faced with an attack is to slow down, or even worse freeze with fear, doing this puts you directly at the mercy of your attacker. In order to avoid this you need to learn how to speed up your reaction time to an altercation. Many of us hesitate when presented with unfamiliar situations, but we can train ourselves to avoid this indecision. One of the best ways to do so is to present yourself with as many unfamiliar and even slightly dangerous situations as you can in order to take the edge off when the real danger arises.

I know it sounds completely ridiculous, but you can really increase your reaction time just by running down the street barefoot, feeling all of those sharp objects underfoot puts you in real time reaction mode, to where you have to move fast in order to keep from being stuck! It may not be the most pleasant of training sessions, but running barefoot really will increase your reaction time in a real hurry!

In order to protect yourself form the blows of an attacking assailant you will have to learn how to block. Even if you have never been in a fight in your life, you should learn how to block an attack if anyone is bold enough to some day attempt to start on with you. Going back to the first self defense strategy mentioned in this chapter, you are going to need good reaction time in order to successfully parry a blow, so make sure your reflexes are up to par.

Once your timing is right, start thinking of different parts of your body as your own built in shields. And your number one build in shield is going to be your forearm. If you see a fist heading your way, throw your forearm up in front of you to block the blow. The second you deflect this attack it throws your enemy off guard, and gives you the perfect opportunity to counterattack. Keep it up and your attacker will soon be put out of commission.

Learn how to Pack a Punch

Packing a punch, means knowing how to turn your fist into a missile aimed right at your would-be assailants head. The first thing you need to know in order to do this, is how to make a fist in the first place. Although for some it is only natural, if you have no experience fighting you may not know how to make a proper fist. So let me explain. The only real way to make a fist is to close your fingers tightly together with your thumb tightly packed in along side your knuckles.

It's important to always make sure your thumb is on the outside of your fist, rather than inside. Otherwise you could end up jamming your thumb really bad (or even breaking it) from the pressure of colliding into your attacker's head. Keep a firm grip, with your thumb on the outside, and slam it as hard as you can into your attacker's face. As they say, the best defense is a good offense, so learn to pack a mean punch and let them have it!

Aggressively Scream

When being attacked out of nowhere it is quite naturally for us to scream with fear, but unless there is someone nearby to hear our cries of distress, this really isn't going to help us. And if our attacker is sadistic enough, screams of pain, sadness, and fear will only encourage them further. But if you were to scream with real menace and aggression at your assailant this could change things completely.

When confronted in that dark alleyway, take any fear you may have and turn it into complete unbridled rage. If someone pulls a knife on you and you scream at your assailant, "I'll tear you apart!" I guarantee you that he will have much more pause than a scream of; "Please don't hurt me!" would ever bring him! Screaming can be an effective means of dissuading an enemy, the key however is how it is you do the screaming. Be bold, aggressive, loud, and strong challenging the would-be attacker to back down.

Psyche Out Your Assailant with a Running Attack

Running away is quite natural. It is the other half of the fight or flight response, and attackers expect people to try to run and get away. But what they do not expect is for someone to run a few feet, stop, turn around and run back at them with a vicious attack! This move is so unexpected that you can completely devastate any would-be attacker.

Lead an attacker on a fake chase, get a good distance from them, then suddenly turn around and fly right at them at full speed, then grab them by the shoulders using all of your speed and momentum to slam them to the ground, and start mercilessly beating the crap out of them until they either give up, or become incapacitated.

<u>**_Inflict Pain with Pressure Points_**</u>

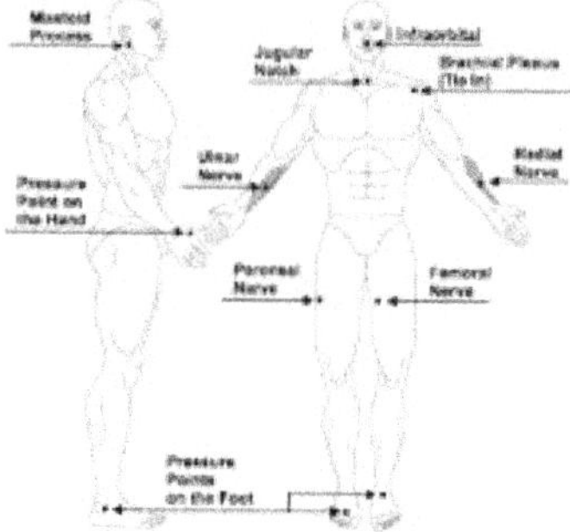

We all have points of pressure distributed throughout our body that when struck can lead to some pretty painful results. The best pressure point you can hit, that will disable an opponent, is on the outside of the upper leg, right between the hips and knees. If you kick someone hard enough in this spot the assailant's entire leg will collapse from underneath them as they fall to the ground in agony.

Conclusion: You can Survive

There is without a doubt that we live in a dangerous world, but if you take all of the strategies of this book and put them to use, you will not have any problem in surviving them. I hope that this book and your own willpower will give you all you need, so that you know, that you *can survive*.

FREE Bonus Reminder

If you have not grabbed it yet, please go ahead and download your special bonus E book *"Chakras for Beginners. 7 Steps To Understand And Balance Chakras, Radiate Energy, And Strengthen Aura"*.

Simply Click the Button Below

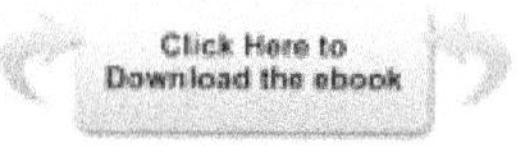

OR Go to This Page

http://lifehacksworld.com/free

BONUS #2: More Free & Discounted Books & Products

Do you want to receive more Free/Discounted Books or Products?

We have a mailing list where we send out our new Books or Products when they go free or with a discount on Amazon. Click on the link below to sign up for Free & Discount Book & Product Promotions.

=> Sign Up for Free & Discount Book & Product Promotions <=

OR Go to this URL

http://zbit.ly/1WBb1Ek